the girl who couldn't stop giving

Bridget Kei

BookLeaf Publishing

India | USA | UK

Presentation by *BookLeaf Publishing*

Web: www.bookleafpub.com

E-mail: info@bookleafpub.com

ISBN: 9789363314276

First edition 2024

*this is dedicated to the underdogs, the outcasts, to anyone
who has ever felt devastatingly alone. to those who have
had no choice but to claw their way out of the darkness.*

you are loved. you are loved. you are loved.

you are light.

TRIGGER WARNING

This poetry collection contains mature themes covering various aspects of complex trauma and mental illness. Please proceed with caution and be sure to prioritize your own mental health—most importantly, know that you are never alone in your struggles.

Thank you ♡

to find the light, you must embrace the dark

she has 2 legs, 2 arms
10 fingers and 10 toes
a beating heart and breathing lungs
yet she still doesn't feel whole

one of her first lessons in life
was to pack up the pain
& bury it into the deepest parts of herself
so she'd never have to feel it again

but when she numbed the dark,
she also numbed the light
until she was a sad shade of gray

when she got older,
she decided her favorite color was yellow
because it was the opposite
of how she had always felt

she wanted to be yellow.

don't get too close,
they say
she'll destroy you
like she's destroyed herself

don't get too close,
they say
she'll want to know you
better than she knows herself

so they stay away
and she believes them
as her yellow fades to gray

she taught herself
how to live
hungry of happiness

when she grew up
she didn't even realize
she was starving.

the mean girls snicker
in an attempt to burn out her fire

little do they know
they're the ones rekindling it

on the first floor of my house
lay a blanket of tension
so thick
it could suffocate me

and on some days,
it does

silencing my voice
stealing my breath

until I don't know
if I'll ever be able to exhale again

I'm beginning to learn
that the biggest wolves
are just sheep in disguise.

how can you hurt without learning to hurt first?
how can you truly love
when you've never felt true love before?

hate is easy.
hate takes you to the trenches
makes you comfortable there,
and it convinces you that it's better that way.

love is terrifying.
it's diving head first.
it's a free fall into a giant abyss of the unknown.

nothing hurts more than vulnerability, yet nothing
destroys you more than refusing to be vulnerable.

vulnerability is the secret. it is necessary.
it is the antidote to shame,
and the key to love.

"put out your own fire,"
they sneer
as they burn her alive

once again,
the weight

came crashing down
on her shoulders

she didn't even flinch.

she sought evidence of their remorse
they smiled back at her,
her bleeding heart mangled between their teeth

trauma hides in sneaky places

it hides in the dusty corners of your bedroom
and the musty mountains of laundry
that sneer at you when you're too drained to clean

it hides in the clench of your jaw,
the bite of your fingernails
and the torn journal pages
you tear stained at 14

the hurt harbors
in the ache in your chest
and the sink of your stomach
when you've had one drink too many

the places you turn to
& the places you turn away from

that's where trauma hides

she grew up in
the calm, centered eye
of a twister

unrelentingly unphased
by the destruction and chaos
swirling around her

forgive her
for trying to grasp onto the wreckage

it is all she has ever known.

forgive her
for screaming at the sky

her voice has never been loud enough.

forgive her
for the storm

she too wishes she was surrounded
by a calm, quiet warmth.

in another life
I was born
with tiny little wings
I'd eventually use to take flight

but in this one
my back was born bare

in this one
I've broken all of my bones
to build everyone else
their very own pair

I don't want to be angry anymore
but it's hard
when I deserved so much more

sometimes I imagine a world
where you borrow love
like a library book

you'd check someone out, and stay a little while

discovering their stories
page by page
word by word
chapter by chapter

you would climb to their peaks
and crumble to their lows
until the moment you run out of pages
and their time is due.

you would return them, gently & carefully
knowing you appreciated every single chapter,
their story etched into your heart forever

the pages would be crisp and clean
no tear stains, no spilled coffee

almost like you were never there to begin with

because you are simply a borrower of their heart
soon to be checked out again

in a haze of dream and sleep
the ticking afternoon clock has just struck three

the summer sun warms our cheeks
relieved only by the slight breeze

I am cradled into you
and you into me

we turn pages upon pages
marked with pencil and pen

we turn the words over on our tongues
and then our tongues over in our mouths

suddenly
the morning hits five-thirty
and you are gone

I thought I knew love
until I discovered my own heart
beating outside of my body

If you were to be mine, and I were to be yours,
you would still be yours
and I would still be mine

but we'd also have this beautiful space
that is ours

a space
where I melt into you
and you melt into me

a space where everything is complete

where I'd squeeze the stress out of your hands
and kiss the sleep out of your eyes

we'd lay
and let our secrets soak
into the sacred air above us
while our bodies baptize
the holy ground beneath us

if you were to be mine and I were to be yours
you'd still be yours
I'd still be mine

but we'd both be ours

my eyes were ablaze
with angry sparks

but I swear,
my soul was as saccharine
as the sweet tears
of the maple tree
we both wept beneath

you ran
I ran

we both ran

until we finally collapsed
into one singular heap

one of the hardest people
I've had to forgive

is the version of myself
that loved you

I saw you last night
and you cut me open again

our hearts spilled fresh blood
as we sat in your car
half strangers, half soulmates
trying to fit the puzzle pieces
of our lives back together

tension became thick as smoke
as we hotboxed the air
with our heartbreak

exchanging breaths of desperation
trying to stop the withdrawals
with the very drug that we craved

trying to comfort
what we both knew we couldn't

we kissed, like we had a million times before
but our lips were foreign

still, we clung to each other
to the past
knowing that when we let go
it was eternal

I didn't want you to hold me anymore

there'd be no point
I had to hold myself anyway

it'll make your heart hurt worse
when she doesn't taste like me
and her hips don't move in cadence with yours

when she doesn't know your sweet spots
and each breath is a guessing game

you'll realize when it's over
that you can't heal a broken heart
by etching in new scars

is it too much to ask
to be held
without being crushed?

cold, where it was once warm
distant, where we were once close
unforgiving, where I have forgiven

I do not know when things went wrong
but I've been here before.

apologizing until my throat bleeds
surrendering until I've made myself small
trapped in a tangled spiral of thoughts

trying to grasp onto what I know
does not want me

let go, I tell myself, but I cannot
my knuckles are white
from hanging on so tight

I want to love what does not love me

so I hurt, again and again
and I apologize, again and again

and I make myself smaller and smaller
until I cease to exist
and there's no one to blame
but myself

stone cold,
she shatters

plummeting from the pedestal
she could never truly reach

one that was high above
any source of heat

gratefully,
she descends
embracing each flame

simply thankful
to be warm again

you've crawled into my bones
you've sat in my skin

yet you don't know me
you haven't met the new me yet

let us waltz through
the house of our heartbreak

spin me sweetly around the shattered glass
and I'll pirouette past our problems

we'll move through the misunderstandings
float under the taunting leaks in the ceiling
and over the angry cracks in the wooden floor

pull me closer and closer
until we're out the door

twirl me into the hopeful twilight
beyond the breaking back porch

I'm not sure where we'll go next
but I know it's somewhere
we haven't danced before

a fallen angel
lay still in the snow
f r o z e n
as the world thaws around her

she exhales the last of summer's sweet breath
and inhales the bitter chill of winter

the frost first bites her,
then it ignites her

she melts into the luminescent pools
that surround her

they swallow her whole
and she sinks into the cold, dark comfort
of what she's always known

"my heart is beating, my lungs are breathing,"
she takes inventory

"but am I living?"

after the last shatter
she packed away her heart

"It's just way too fragile,"
she whispered

as the beat in her chest
turned blue

I've started to think that abandonment
will follow me wherever I go

maybe I will always drown in my thoughts
sinking beneath rushing waves
silently screaming for help

maybe I dug my own grave
did I shut out anyone
who would plunge into deep water for me?

I'm starting to think I attract those
that want to push me into the dark sea
and hold my head under
until my lungs burst
but maybe it's more beautiful
where there is no light
only darkness
only peace

I've been treading water for so long
my legs are getting tired

I think I might let myself
s i n k

he asked me if I wanted a shot of espresso

I smiled weakly and replied
"no thank you."

I'm the kind of tired
caffeine could never fix

when I glow
people assume I've spent my life
basking in the bright, beautiful sun

in reality,
I've had to master photosynthesis

my only option
was to create strength
from the light I could find around me

I guess you're good at that sort of thing
when you know the darkness well enough
to have to teach yourself
how to stop craving it

I ripped out
the writhing wound
aching in my chest

it fought and it fought
with each raw, reeling breath

I covered it in love
said thank you
and laid it to rest

as day breaks
and darkness falls

she creeps into her coffin
dark and hollow as she crawls

she has learned to make a home here
in the sadness, in the grief
in the sweet feeling of relief

she feels much more secure
beneath the ground
than above it

the dirt shields her from the scalding sunlight
as a smile crosses her lips

nothing could be more suffocating
than the hell of humanity
that treads above her

she wishes the world goodbye
as her breath dissolves beneath the earth

at last,
for the first time
she is at peace

my grief is outweighed by relief
it feels so good to know
that you can't destroy me any longer

after the catastrophe
she packed up her things
& left everything behind

she left the things she loved
right there in the wreckage

there was a time
she thought maybe, just maybe
they had love for her too

that they could see beyond
the guard she held so tight
& realize she just felt small, full of fright

her heart began to rot when she realized
they had slammed the door
to the fallout shelter
and left her there

she trembles as she looks back
ahead of her, the sky is a bright blue
the storm is finally over

loving yourself
does not always look like
bubble baths, face masks, and a glass of wine

sometimes you have to reach
into the graveyard of skeletons
that clutter the empty space within your heart

bones clanking,
whispering *"you are not enough."*

sometimes self-love
is facing your demons head-on
horns sharp
pointed right at you

sometimes it's letting out painful sobs,
the kind that has you convinced
your ribcage might break in two

sometimes healing
is more than just a good book
and a cup of chamomile tea

sometimes it's bleeding yourself dry
so you can fill yourself back up

I ripped each bloodied bandage off
and let in the sweet, sweet air

once healed
each wound revealed
something raw and rare

in the startling dark
the light began to pour out
of every tedious crack
in her gentle heart

may your eyes leak
all of the tears
you could not shed before

the ones that wait like tensed water
about to burst out of a flooded door

may you crack the dismal dam
of your aching heart wide open
and let your feelings pour

may you find sweet relief
in the ritual of being sore

they called her *lightning*
the way she could alchemize
her angry electricity
into pure love and light

doubt and anger
swallowed her whole

it was in this dark hell
that she would silently stew

when it finally spit her out
she was covered in wounds

but she was bright,
she was light
and she was brand new

fractures of radiant, golden light
shine brightest
through shards of shattered glass
— *hikari*

when no one wants to understand you,
keep your head high.
you understand yourself.

when they tell you no one will ever love you,
place your hand on your heart
and wholeheartedly love yourself.

when the world wants to shame you,
blame you, and berate you
breathe in,
breathe out
and love yourself even harder.

they have not walked a day in your shoes.
they have not spent a second in your head.
they know nothing about you.

when you don't want to be here,
get up
and show up for yourself.
be more present than you ever have before.

you deserve to be here.

quiet the world around you
to discover the world within you

you seek beauty in the pigment of your new blush,
and the way it flushes your cheeks
the perfect shade of peach

you seek beauty in the scale that sneers at you,
a perfect image out of reach

you seek beauty in the ugliest parts of society
claiming them as the broken parts of yourself

please promise me
that instead

you'll seek beauty in the sunset
and the way it lights your eyes golden

you'll seek beauty within your soul
and the things at which it leaps

promise me

you'll seek beauty in the eternal,
unwavering parts of yourself

instead of the falsities
that can be bought on a shelf

you are not falling behind
you are just beginning to align

I feel a part of myself calling out to me, gently yelling
"yes, this is you. it's been you all along."

you love bookstores, the smell of fresh paper
and the crisp turn of a brand-new page

you breathe a sweet sigh of relief when you pour
your heart out in the form of words

you buy too many journals,
swearing you'll fill up every single one (you never do)

you crave warmth in bubble baths, hot tea, or a good hug
the way you feel everything so deeply bothers you
but deep down, you know it's a superpower

music rocks you to sleep and nestles you in protection
as you delve deep into the lyrics, unraveling the meaning
of each word—questioning every syllable, marking what
it means to you

one day, someone will know these details & they will
truly realize what they mean

they will not take them for granted. they will cherish
them with their entire heart & soul. and at last,
you will feel understood

I've come to realize that moments
are as fleeting
and as fragile
as the monarchal wings of a butterfly

they bloom
nestled in a warm cocoon
until they're ready to take flight

as much as you may want to hold on
to each beautiful memory,

you have to let go
say goodbye
wish them well

& thank them for the time you had
because without them
you would not have been transformed.

you may be little me,
and I may be older you,
but we are not the same.

your heart is softer
your voice booms louder
your eyes shine brighter
your smile stretches wider

bold, brave, unafraid
you exist in authenticity

I guess that's the difference between you and I,
between then and now,
I've morphed into a million versions
of what others have wanted me to be.

deep down, we remain the same
yet I have so much to learn from you

you love without limits
and give without expectation

it'll take a while before you realize that is your power

I will return to you
I promise
I'm returning to you

ACKNOWLEDGEMENTS

to my dad, who gave me the life and the creativity that I am so incredibly grateful for. without you, we would have never stayed afloat. thank you for working long hours to make sure we had food on the table and for doing your best, always.

to my mom, my true rock and the strongest woman I know—I would not have survived without you. thank you for always putting us first, for bleeding for us, for taking on my pain when it had nowhere else to go. I am so proud of the person you are. you deserve the world.

to my sister and best friend, Emily, and my brother-in-law, Mike, for continuing to bring light and laughter to my life—always. for making me smile when no one else could. I will forever be thankful for your presence in my life, for giving me endless amounts of wisdom, for being there for me through thick, thin, and everything in between.

to my wonderful brother, Brandon and my sister-in-law, Katie, for constantly being a source of stability and strength. for always showing up and giving me a place to go, no matter the circumstance. for being incredible parents.

to my niece, Celine, your little light has already given the world so much. I'm so grateful to watch you grow and so proud of each step you take. I know you're going to continue to evolve into someone so incredibly great.

to my unicorns, Ellen and Rejean, your safe space has meant more to me than you'll ever know. I will forever and always cherish the strength; the vulnerability; the authenticity; the pure, sweet light that you hold.

to my Grandma Bea, my aunt Mary, and the rest of my incredibly beautiful extended family in the US and in Japan—you are all so special and carry such unique talents and strengths. thank you for everything.

to my beautiful, genuine friends who have been there for me through it all—thank you. you mean so much to me. thank you.

to every person who showed me even an ounce of kindness, forgiveness, education, or wisdom throughout my journey, thank you. I will carry the lessons you've taught me forever.

and to little Bridget, you did it. you really did it. our dream of becoming an author came true. I'm so proud of you.